KU-686-080

CONTENTS

CHAPTER 1

BEARING WITNESS TO WAR

The Syrian **civil war** has been called the biggest **humanitarian** and **refugee** crisis of our time. What began in early 2011 as a series of small protests against the Syrian government, has turned into a deadly conflict between warring **factions** across the country. Now entering its seventh year, the war has killed nearly half a million people, and more than 11 million have been forced to flee their homes.

At first, the war was fought between soldiers who support Syria's president, Bashar al-Assad, and a group of **defecting** soldiers and ordinary **civilians** (known as rebels) who oppose his power. As the war intensified, many other warring factions have joined the conflict. Now half of Syria's pre-war population has been **displaced**, or forced to leave their homes. Many Syrian refugees, and those who remain, are in desperate need of humanitarian aid. Families are struggling to survive in war-torn Syria or to make a new home in neighbouring countries. Others have risked their lives to travel to Europe. They do not know when they will return to peacetime Syria or if they will return at all.

Syria's civil war has brought destruction and danger to people's lives. Millions have now fled the country in search of safety.

Technology has played a major part in the war in Syria, with social media informing the world of many important events.

The Syrian civil war has become known as the first social media war. No other conflict has been covered in such detail or reported so widely across the globe, by ordinary people as well as news reporters. Today, anyone with a smartphone, internet access and a desire to share their experiences can reach out to the world through YouTube, Twitter and other social media. These communication channels have had both a positive and negative impact on the crisis. Social media has been used to gather support for the revolution and to inform fighters of strategic plans. It has also been used to influence how the conflict is portrayed and perceived by the wider world. Thousands of videos have been posted online, causing outrage and concern over alleged atrocities on both sides. These posts have also raised the difficulty of discerning the truth from **propaganda**, with all sides using social media to promote their cause. Syria has become a dangerous place for journalists. More than 100 have been killed during the conflict, and so news agencies increasingly rely on social media for important updates. Social media has become invaluable for those inside Syria as well as those on the outside attempting to work out what is going on.

Syria is a small country bordering Turkey, Iraq, Jordan, Lebanon, Israel and occupied Palestinian territory. A land of fertile plains, rugged mountains and dry deserts, it is also a nation full of rich political and cultural history. Its capital, Damascus, and the largest city, Aleppo, are among the oldest continuously inhabited cities in the world. Full of ancient mosques (Muslim places of worship), Roman ruins, and castles dating from the **Crusades**, Syria and the surrounding area has long been known as the "cradle of civilization". Syria's rich and varied past has also brought a wealth of religions and **ethnicities** to the nation. The majority of Syrians, about 87 per cent, are Muslim. For generations, they have been living side-by-side with Christians, Jews, Kurds and Yazidis, for example. These diverse communities have managed to overlook many of their differences. However, when unrest threatened the country in 2011, both sides of the conflict began to manipulate these natural divisions.

In 1946, in the aftermath of World War II (1939–1945), Syria gained independence from France. In the decades that followed, different groups fought for power, destabilizing the country. Then, in 1971, Hafez al-Assad became president. At first, all was well. The country stabilized and developed good relations with the United States and other leading nations. However, the Assad government was an

Damascus is one of the oldest cities in the world. People have lived there for more than 11,000 years. Once filled with bustling marketplaces, it has now largely been reduced to rubble.

authoritarian regime, tightly controlled by the president, with important positions given to loyal aides. In 1982, for example, Hafez ordered the Syrian Army (under the command of his brother) to besiege the town of Hama to dispel an anti-government uprising by the Muslim Brotherhood. The Muslim Brotherhood is an Islamic religious, political and social movement. Much of the city was destroyed, and reports suggest up to 40,000 civilians were killed.

Unlike democratic nations, the Syrian people were not allowed to vote for their leader. When Hafez died in 2000, his son, Bashar, became president. Today, the al-Assad family has been in power for more than 40 years. A new leader gave Syrians hope that things could change, but people became increasingly angry when Bashar failed to deliver long-promised reforms. Then in December 2010, a wave of protests and demands for change rose around the Middle East and North Africa, known as the Arab Spring. In Tunisia, President Zine El Abidine Ben Ali was overthrown, and the Egyptian president Hosni Mubarak also fell from power. These successful uprisings gave hope to neighbouring countries, such as Syria, Yemen, Bahrain and Libya, that they could fight for democracy.

These posters show President Bashar al-Assad, whose family has been in power for more than four decades. Many of his relatives hold government positions.

7

In Syria, the unrest began in early 2011. An important protest took place in March, for example, in the city of Deraa. When 15 school children were arrested for writing anti-government graffiti on a wall in the city, local people protested for their release. There were claims that some of the children had been tortured, and one of them, 13-year-old Hamza al-Khateeb, had been killed. At first, the protests were peaceful. People wanted to see the children freed, but they were also protesting at the way President Assad was running the country. They wanted democracy and greater freedom for people in Syria. They were frustrated by the government's economic policies, too. A severe drought in Syria from 2007 to 2010 had caused more than one million people to migrate (move) from the countryside to the cities, leading to increased poverty, unemployment and social unrest.

Assad's government responded angrily to the protests. On 18 March, the Syrian Army fired on demonstrators, killing four people. Many others were arrested. People were shocked and angry at the way they were being treated, and protests had spread to other parts of the country, too. By July, an opposition group called the Free Syrian Army (FSA) had formed and began fighting back. The group was made up of army officers and soldiers who had defected to protect the civilians opposing Assad's rule. They became known as rebel fighters, and many ordinary people joined them. Initially, the rebel fighters were weak, with few weapons and not much manpower. It was only natural that they sought coalitions with other anti-government groups. Unfortunately, some volatile and extreme opposition groups joined in the fray, and before long, the country was sliding into civil war. There have been reports of up to one thousand different opposition groups since the conflict began, with an estimated 100,000 fighters.

Some rebel fighters were army soldiers who opposed the government.

EY

Discarded

CIVIL WAR

KATIE DICKER

Raintree is an imprint of Capstone Global Library Limited, a company incorporated in England and Wales having its registered office at 264 Banbury Road, Oxford, OX2 7DY - Registered company number: 6695582

www.raintree.co.uk
myorders@raintree.co.uk

Produced for Raintree by Calcium
Editor for Calcium: Sarah Eason
Designer for Calcium: Paul Myerscough
Designer for Raintree: Cynthia Della-Rovere
Picture research by Rachel Blount
Production by Katy LaVigne
Printed and bound in India

ISBN 978 1 4747 6586 2 (hardback)
22 21 20 19 18
10 9 8 7 6 5 4 3 2 1

ISBN 978 1 4747 6601 2 (paperback)
23 22 21 20 19
10 9 8 7 6 5 4 3 2 1

British Library Cataloguing in Publication Data
A full catalogue record for this book is available from the British Library.

Acknowledgements
We would like to thank the following for permission to reproduce photographs:
Cover: Wikimedia Commons: Zyzzzzzy; Inside: Dept. of Defense: US Air Force photo by Senior Airman Erin Trower/Released 19; Dreamstime: Richard Harvey 8; Shutterstock: Aaron Amat 12, ART production 4, 27, 29, 38, Homo Cosmicos 34, Sfio Cracho 5, Suha Derbent 6, Evan El-Amin 35, Fpolat69 14, Jorg Hackemann 31, Kafeinkolik 17, 25, Thomas Koch 9, 23, Sergey Kohl 30, Stacey Newman 40, Owen_Holdaway 21, Procyk Radek 24, Railway fx 16, Rawpixel.com 41, Serkan Senturk 7, Tolga Sezgin 37, Evgenii Sribnyi 18, Syda Productions 13, ZouZou 1, 22; © UNHCR/Bassam Diab: 28, 32, 33, 36, 44–45; Wikimedia Commons: Abkhazian Network News Agency 10, Agência Brasil Fotografias 39, Defend International 20, Ggia 26, Kurdishstruggle 15, US Department of State, US Mission Photo/Eric Bridiers 42, Photo by Bertil Videt 11, Voice of America 43.

EYEWITNESS

People from all walks of life took part in peaceful protests against the Syrian government in 2011.

In 2011, a man called Abdulhamid took part in peaceful protests against the actions of the Syrian government in his hometown of Damascus. He was proud to be part of an uprising known in Arabic as *Thawret al-Karameh*, which means "Revolution of Dignity". He could not have foreseen that, a year later, he would be forced to flee his homeland and become a refugee living in Turkey. He said:

"When Syrians first took to the streets in civil protest, it was to lobby for human rights, political rights, freedom of speech and freedom of the press. In the beginning, these were the basic demands. But radicalization has moved the focus of the battle away from getting rid of the authoritarian regime. And we still have the same regime in Damascus."

Why do you think Abdulhamid uses the term "civil protest"?

What are some of the human rights that people were protesting for?

Do you think everyone wanted to get rid of the authoritarian regime? Why not?

How do you think people felt when the focus of the war changed?

CHAPTER 2

DESCENT INTO CIVIL WAR

By July 2012, the violence in Syria had become so widespread that the International Red Cross declared that the country was in a state of civil war. People wanted President Assad to resign, but he refused. As the violence became worse, Assad offered some changes to the way the country was governed, but people found it difficult to believe his promises.

The violence escalated as rebel groups fought government troops for control of cities, towns and villages. Fighting reached Damascus and Aleppo. In Damascus, the rebels initially gained significant ground, capturing six districts. They also killed four top government ministers (including the defence minister and President Assad's brother-in-law) when a rebel bomb went off in a government building. Despite these strong beginnings, however, the rebels were forced to **retreat** when the government retaliated with **air strikes**. This was the first time that helicopters, bombers, tanks, troops and gunmen had been used in central Damascus. The city had become a war zone.

° A government soldier takes aim against rebel fighters during the "Battle for Damascus".

Some middle-class Syrians support President Assad and the continuity that comes with his governance. Others fear the consequences of opposing his power.

By August, the government had claimed victory in the "Battle for Damascus". They also began a campaign of **collective punishment** against civilians in the city who had supported the Free Syrian Army. They wanted to drive the rebels completely out of Damascus. A year later, rebel groups began targeting the capital again. Meanwhile, the struggle for Aleppo continued. This was just the start of what would become a four-year **siege** of the city. According to the **United Nations (UN)**, by June 2013, 90,000 people had been killed in Syria. By August 2015, this figure had almost tripled to 250,000. Despite international calls for peace efforts, the war showed no signs of abating.

The UN condemned the use of weapons in civilian areas and declared that **war crimes** had been committed during the conflict. Although the country was in chaos, President Assad still had supporters in Syria. Some middle-class Syrians preferred him to the opposition. They had benefited from his reforms and applauded his anti-corruption measures. President Assad was also a "well-known brand". Some Syrians preferred the safety of continuity that decades of Assad rule had brought to the nation, and resisted change that might bring negative influences. However, many were showing their support in fear of what would happen if they opposed Assad's rule.

There have been reports of chemical weapons being used by both sides in the Syrian civil war. Chemical weapons are poisonous gases or other chemicals used in conflict. They are designed to affect a lot of people over a large area. Chemical weapons were first used on soldiers in World War I (1914–1918), but after this war, their use was banned under international law because their impact was so devastating. The effects of chemical weapons can vary according to the type. Some cause horrific burns and blisters on the skin. Others make it difficult to breathe. Under the Chemical Weapons Convention, 188 countries have agreed to ban the use and production of chemical weapons, but seven countries, including Syria, have not signed this deal.

The world's attention was turned to the use of chemical weapons in Syria in August 2013, when opposition groups reported a suspected **sarin** attack in Ghouta, Damascus. Online videos showed images of men, women and children choking and convulsing (suffering from spasms), as well as the bodies of victims. Later, it became apparent that more than 1,400

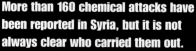

More than 160 chemical attacks have been reported in Syria, but it is not always clear who carried them out.

The presidents of the United States and Russia agreed a deal that put an end to Syria's stockpile of chemical weapons.

people had been killed. The Syrian government denied it was behind the attack, blaming it on extreme rebel groups. A few days later, the Syrian government granted UN weapons inspectors access to the site. They found "clear and convincing evidence that surface-to-surface rockets containing the nerve agent sarin were used." A later report said that the quality and quantity of the sarin used suggested it was from the Syrian military, together with the expertise and equipment needed to carry out the attack.

In February 2017, the Syrian-American Medical Society (SAMS) said that nearly 1,500 people had been killed in 161 chemical weapons attacks in the Syrian conflict, while another 15,000 had been injured. There were also reports of the use of other weapons, such as **napalm** and bombs containing chlorine gas.

While the world reeled in shock, it waited to see how other countries would respond. The United States was reluctant to become involved in another conflict in the region after lengthy and costly wars in Iraq and Afghanistan. Politicians from the United Kingdom voted against military action. However, in September 2013, the United States and Russia persuaded President Assad to agree to a plan to destroy Syria's chemical weapons, to avoid the prospect of US air strikes in retaliation. The Organization for the Prohibition of Chemical Weapons (OPCW) was instructed to destroy Syria's chemical weapons, in a bid to prevent further atrocities. A month later, the **Nobel Peace Prize** was awarded to the OPCW for its ongoing work in Syria as well as 16 years of efforts worldwide to eliminate chemical weapons.

The Kurds are the largest ethnic minority group in Syria, making up about one-tenth of the population. For many years, they have been seeking **political autonomy** for the Kurdish inhabited areas of northern Syria, or outright independence as part of Kurdistan. However, things changed on 7 October 2011, when Mashaal Tammo, a Syrian politician who campaigned for Kurdish rights, was shot by men believed to be government agents. The next day, when mourners gathered for his funeral, the Syrian Army fired on them, killing five people. Since then, protests for Kurdish independence have become part of the wider Syrian uprising.

In July 2012, President Assad withdrew most of his troops from the north, claiming they were needed to fight the FSA in other cities. Kurdish **militias**, known as the People's Protection Units, took control of the region, renaming it Rojava. Today, the Kurds are fighting Islamic State (IS), too (see page 16), and hundreds of Kurdish women have joined the struggle. In 2014, the Women's Protection Units, an all-female offshoot of the People's Protection Units, grew to more than 7,000 fighters. These female soldiers are testament to the Syrian's resolve to fight for social justice and political freedom, as part of a more personal quest for the oppressed people of Kurdistan.

Kurds celebrate a religious festival in Qamlo, Syria, under the watchful eye of a Syrian Army helicopter.

EYEWITNESS

Reports say that women now make up 36 per cent of those fighting IS in Syria.

As a seven-year-old schoolboy, Shafiq was not allowed to speak the Kurdish language in his lessons. Unable to speak a word of Arabic, he was forced to quickly adapt to his surroundings. Shafiq now campaigns on behalf of Kurdish refugees. He says:

"As Kurds, we have our own culture, language and traditions. For over a century, we have been trying to remember and retain our heritage, because we are not allowed to practise these basic rights. Our dream is to have 'Kurdistan' back in our own hands and the freedom to live as Kurds, no longer fearing persecution and being forced to use another nation's language."

How would you feel if your native language was banned on a daily basis?

How would you remember and retain traditions while living in fear of persecution?

Why might the Kurds' identity be more difficult to keep with each passing decade?

CHAPTER 3

THE BLACK FLAG OF TERROR

As the Syrian crisis has continued, multiple wars are now at play. The original struggle for political freedom and social justice has brought the involvement of regional and international powers. More alarmingly, however, a war of conquest by **extremist** groups has also joined the fray.

In 2014, over the border in neighbouring Iraq, the terrorist group IS began to take over large areas of the country. The group quickly gathered recruits using the internet and social media to entice followers and to spread fear. IS is an extremist Muslim group based mainly in Iraq and Syria, where it claims to have 10,000 fighters from across the globe. Also known as Daesh, ISIS and ISIL, the group has extreme religious beliefs and uses brutal violence against anyone who fails to follow its strict rules. It also demands that other extremist Islamic groups accept its supreme authority. In June 2014, the group rebranded to become "Islamic State" and declared itself a worldwide **caliphate**, claiming religious, political and military authority over all Muslims worldwide. However, the group's violent beliefs could not be further

Islamic State has gained power in northern and eastern Syria. The group flies a black flag, inscripted with a declaration of Islamic faith, to boast of its territories.

from what the majority of Muslims believe. IS announced the city of Raqqa to be the headquarters of its caliphate in Syria.

In Syria, IS was able to capitalize on the chaos and instability of war to claim land and power. The group initially supported the opposition, sending funds and fighters, but the rebels condemned the group's brutal tactics. IS soon began conducting ground attacks on both government forces and rebel groups. By the end of 2015, IS controlled a vast area of western Iraq and northern and eastern Syria, with a population of up to 8 million people. Soon government forces and rebel groups had to fight a separate, simultaneous war against IS in the region. For some Syrians, especially young people growing up in times of violence and despair, extremist groups such as IS have filled a vacuum in their lives, captivating vulnerable minds and encouraging people to commit to their cause. Others have been captured by IS and forced to convert or die.

IS is believed to be the world's wealthiest militant group, with access to funds of around £1.5 billion. The money comes from a variety of sources, making it very difficult for international powers to cut off their financing. Income comes from the sale of oil, taxation, donations, **extortion** and ransom payments, for example. IS fighters also have a wealth of weaponry at their disposal and have been known to capture tanks and armoured vehicles from the Syrian and Iraqi armies.

In times of civil war, other countries may try to intervene to stop the fighting. Now entering its seventh year, the war in Syria has seen several interventions from foreign powers attempting to ease the conflict. However, not all countries can agree on who is to blame. The US, UK and Turkey are just some of the nations expressing support for the rebel fighters. Meanwhile, Russia, Iran and Iraq, for example, are backing the Syrian regime. Governments show their support for a particular side by offering funding, supplying weapons and equipment, training fighters, sending military advisers, or launching military campaigns and air strikes (rebel groups are not known to have the capacity for air power, for example). It has been argued in recent years, however, that sending weapons is no way to end the war, especially if the weapons fall into the wrong hands – nobody knows exactly who the "rebels" are.

Many people believe that the international community has not done enough to help the people of Syria. Former US President Barack Obama, for example, referred to the use of chemical weapons as

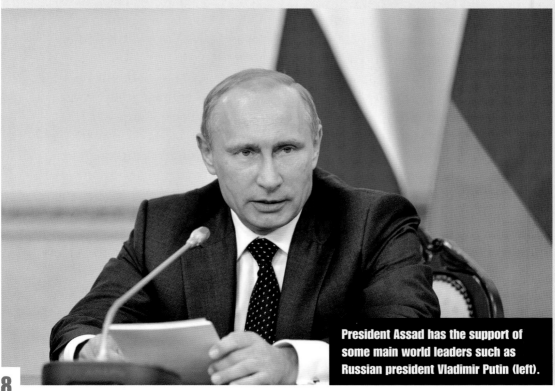

President Assad has the support of some main world leaders such as Russian president Vladimir Putin (left).

A US fighter jet prepares for a mission to carry out air strikes in Iraq and Syria, in a bid to thwart the advance of IS.

a "red line" that would prompt his country to intervene in the conflict. However, when there were allegations of chemical weapons atrocities in 2013, the United States hesitated at military intervention. Whatever their differences, foreign powers have recently united against a more serious, common enemy. Both sides have agreed to make the fight against international terrorism a top priority. However, the definition of "terrorist group" is disputed. While most agree that IS, which has become a violent threat to the global community, should be defeated, President Assad and the countries that support him consider all armed groups that are fighting the Syrian government to be terrorists.

In September 2014, a US-led coalition (including the UK, France, and several Arab countries, such as Jordan and Saudi Arabia) launched a series of air strikes against IS and other extremist groups on the ground in Syria. One year later, Russia began conducting air strikes against "terrorist groups" too. However, many of these attacks struck anti-Assad rebel groups that the West was trying to protect. While air strikes have had some impact on the strength of IS in the region, innocent civilians have been caught up in the destruction. Many people have been killed or forced to flee for safety. Military intervention has also destroyed important infrastructure, such as oil or water supplies, on which people rely for their energy, sanitation and survival. The civilians, whom the international community is trying to support, are also paying the price of their intervention.

The mountainous region of northern Iraq and northeastern Syria is the traditional homeland of a small ethnic minority group called the Yazidi people. After many years of oppression, the Yazidis faced a new threat in 2014 in the form of IS. This extremist group considers the Yazidis to be **infidels** and began capturing Yazidis in Iraq and Syria. In the early hours of 3 August 2014, for example, IS seized control of the Sinjar region of northern Iraq, near the Syrian border, which is home to about 350,000 Yazidi people. IS fighters gave the Yazidis one choice: Convert to Islam or die. Men who were unable to escape were killed, while women and children were taken captive. They were transported to Syria, where they were abused and sold at slave markets. Some Yazidis escaped to the nearby Sinjar Mountains, but they became trapped without food and water, and faced starvation and death. In the days that followed, former US President Barack Obama authorized targeted air strikes on IS forces in the region, and an airdrop of humanitarian aid to the Yazidis on Mount Sinjar. With the assistance of other countries and groups in the area, the majority of the fifty thousand Yazidis who fled to the mountains were **evacuated**.

In June 2016, the UN officially recognized IS's persecution of the Yazidis as "genocide". Genocide is the deliberate killing of a particular group of people. During the August 2014 atrocities alone, approximately 5,000 people were massacred and about 7,000 women and children were taken captive. Around 3,200 Yazidis are still being held by IS, mostly in Syria, and more than 400,000 Yazidi people are now displaced.

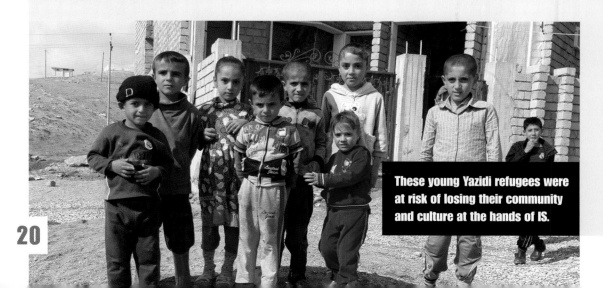

These young Yazidi refugees were at risk of losing their community and culture at the hands of IS.

This Yazidi woman managed to escape from IS and now seeks shelter in a refugee camp. However, many of her friends and family may have been killed or captured.

EYEWITNESS

Nadia Murad was 19 when, one night, IS attacked her Yazidi village. Her mother and six of her brothers were killed, while Nadia and her two sisters were taken captive. After three months of abuse and torture, Nadia escaped and fled to Germany. She has since testified before the UN to raise awareness of the plight of the Iraqi and Syrian people:

"Being a survivor of genocide comes with great responsibility – for I am the lucky one. Having lost my brothers, mother and many more family members and friends, it is a responsibility I embrace fully and take very seriously. My role as an activist is not just about my suffering – it is about a collective suffering. Telling my story and reliving the horrors I encountered is no easy task, but the world must know. The world must feel a moral responsibility to act, and if my story can influence world leaders to act, then it must be told."

What do you think it would have taken for Nadia to survive her ordeal and escape and travel to Germany?

It would have been very painful and upsetting for Nadia to tell her story. Why do you think she wanted to share her story with the world?

Look up what an "activist" is. What influence do you think Nadia could have on world leaders?

CHAPTER 4

FLEEING THE VIOLENCE

When it became clear that there was no immediate resolution to the unrest in Syria, many families began to flee the violence. The decision to leave a home, a job and personal belongings is a difficult one, but many felt they had no choice. They may have witnessed a bombing or seen friends or relatives killed. It was no longer safe to go to work or school – it was time to leave.

When people are forced to leave the country where they live, they become known as refugees. According to the UN, about 11 million Syrians have fled their homes. This includes nearly 5 million refugees who have fled Syria itself in the hope of a better future. They are now the world's largest refugee population. The journey to Syria's border can be as risky as staying behind. Families find themselves walking great distances through unfamiliar terrain and dangerous conditions, with only the belongings they can carry. There are fears of being caught in the crossfire of warring factions. Many

More than fifteen thousand unaccompanied and separated children have crossed Syria's borders since 2011.

Refugees have no choice but to leave their country for fear of what will happen if they remain.

walk under the cover of darkness. Some are young men escaping the threat of compulsory military service because they do not want to fight against their own people. With little money or means, they suffer hunger, thirst and exhaustion. If the weather turns, they have the added burden of heavy rains, mud or snow.

Those who stay behind are also in dire need of assistance. In 2016, for example, the UN said it would need £2.3 billion to help the 13.5 million people inside Syria, half of which are children. About 70 per cent of the population are without access to safe drinking water, one in three people do not have enough to eat,

more than two million children are out of school, and four out of five people live in poverty. Electricity supplies are often cut off, and there is limited access to fuel and medical care. If the dangers of fleeing war were not enough, the risk of dying of starvation or disease is very real. The warring factions in the conflict have also compounded these problems by refusing humanitarian agencies access to civilians in need. In 2015, for example, only 10 per cent of all requests for UN aid convoys to reach the most needy were approved and delivered. As well as besieged town and cities, up to 4.5 million Syrians now live in remote, hard-to-reach areas.

About one-tenth of Syrian refugees are now living in refugee camps. These makeshift settlements have become their homes.

The majority of Syrians have fled to the neighbouring nations of Jordan, Lebanon, Turkey and Iraq. In 2015, for example, Syrian refugees caused Lebanon's population to increase by 25 per cent. As part of the Arab world, these countries share similar languages and customs. Many Syrians have chosen to stay close to the border, to keep a link to their homeland. Some hope to support relief efforts. Syrians may know people in these border countries they can stay with. However, as the crisis drags on, many host families are unable to offer the room or financial support in the long term.

In many border countries, refugee camps have been set up. These safe places offer basic shelter, a place to grow or buy food, and to get safe water. The UN estimates that one in ten Syrian refugees live in camps. Health clinics and schools are sometimes provided, but the camps bring risks, too. The crowded, makeshift settlements have limited water supplies or sanitation, bringing diseases when medical supplies are already low. Winter brings more challenges – shelters leak and tents collapse in the wind.

Many refugees are without heat, electricity or warm clothes. The camps are a source of survival, but many families feel trapped and a long way from home. Making plans for the future is very difficult when you have no home of your own or a job to go to.

Some families find shelter in derelict, abandoned buildings. Syrians have been found living in old barns, cowsheds, chicken coops and storage sheds, with no heat or running water, often paying rent to do so. Others seek shelter in nearby towns, trying to settle and find work in unfamiliar communities. In Jordan and Lebanon, it is illegal for Syrians to work. Refugees struggle to find odd jobs there, and they have to accept low wages that do not cover their most basic needs.

About 10 per cent of the refugees have risked the journey to Europe in the hope of a better life. Some European countries have agreed to accept a fixed number of refugees who want to start a new life there. They apply for **asylum** and are given refugee status. Germany has taken more refugees than any other European nation (more than 420,000 in 2015). However, the journey to Europe is long and dangerous. If Syrians are using transportation, the journey takes from one to three months. If they are walking, it will take much longer. Not all refugees make it across the Mediterranean Sea alive. Those that do still face steep challenges and often disappointment, because much of the route into western Europe has now been closed.

When Syrians flee their homes, they can take only what they can carry.

25

Thousands of Syrian refugees try to reach Europe, where they hope to be granted asylum. After fleeing war-torn Syria, they must first travel to coastal countries such as Turkey and Egypt. When they arrive at their destination, these desperate families arrange transportation with smugglers across the Mediterranean Sea. It is an expensive journey that can cost £1,500 per person. It is also extremely dangerous; by October 2016, 3,740 people had drowned while crossing the Mediterranean. Despite the risks, thousands of refugees make the perilous trip. According to the United Nations High Commissioner for Refugees (UNHCR), 362,376 refugees arrived in Europe by sea in 2016. More than 82,000 fled Syria, most of whom arrived in Greece.

This is just the beginning for refugees hoping to make it to countries such as Germany or Scandinavia. Volunteers and aid workers greet some survivors of the sea crossing with food, blankets and medical care. Once they have regained their strength, refugees are also given vital information for their onward journey. The use of technology has been important in this regard. It has provided translation services, navigation systems and the use of social media to track down lost relatives, to hear from those who have gone on ahead, and to let family and friends know they are safe.

Syrian refugees travel across the sea in small, crowded boats and inflatable rafts.

EYEWITNESS

Fleeing war-torn Syria was a different type of ordeal for Walaa and her three small children. Walaa carried her baby, pushed her toddler in a buggy and walked alongside four-year-old Sami during the physically punishing two-day walk across the border. In Turkey, smugglers promised to transport them to Greece. Walaa and her children eventually found space on a flimsy rubber dinghy. Exhausted and poor, they reached Lesbos just a few days after Macedonia closed its border with Greece (the most common route into Europe). Walaa is still trying to reach her husband in Germany. He left six months before them, in the hope of finding work, because they could not afford for the whole family to make the journey together:

Some children work to help their families raise funds for the journey to Europe. This girl is selling bread on the streets of Damascus.

"It reached the point that I felt that being in the war in Syria is probably even better than walking this route ... [In Turkey] other people went on the boat, but I was kept behind and [the smugglers] told me to clean the house ... they took advantage of me. I spoke to my husband in Germany, and he said to leave that house and go ..."

Why do you think Walaa questioned her choice of leaving war-torn Syria?

Why do you think Macedonia closed its border with Greece?

How do you think Walaa's husband felt when he left his family and travelled to Germany?

27

CHAPTER 5

TRAPPED IN A WAR ZONE

Syrians who have fled their homes for other locations within the country are a group known as "internally displaced people". There are at least six million internally displaced people in Syria, according to the Syrian Centre for Policy Research (SCPR), although other organizations have put this figure higher, at 7.6 million.

The civil war has had a devastating impact on the lives of many ordinary civilians. There is a very real threat of being caught up in the fighting. The sound of shooting and bombing has become a part of everyday life, and there are no safe spaces for children to play or families to function. Homes, hospitals, schools and stores have been reduced to rubble, often with civilians inside. People stay away from school and work to stay safe, but there is no guarantee that home is a safe haven. When the air strikes hit, all they can do is pray.

In addition to the threat of fighting, civilians are facing a shortage of many basic needs. Food and fuel are in short supply, and access to water has been restricted due to bombing

For the families left behind, life is becoming harder than ever.

When a city is under siege, its residents become trapped in a war zone.

or contamination. In December 2016, for example, the water supply was cut off for more than 5 million residents of Damascus. The government said the rebels had contaminated the flow with diesel, while the rebels claimed that government bombs had destroyed the infrastructure. The world has witnessed images of children dying of starvation and people heating plastic from broken chairs and pipes in desperation for fuel.

More than half of hospitals have been partially or completely destroyed, and many doctors have fled the country. According to the United Nations International Children's Emergency Fund (UNICEF), each doctor used to look after the needs of around 600 people, but now each doctor is faced with up to 4,000 patients. There are signs of malnutrition in children,

and waterborne diseases are rife. Medication is already in short supply. Some doctors from Western nations have been offering to help with advice, using Skype from their clinics thousands of kilometres away.

There are reports that government troops have carried out a "surrender or starve" strategy, cutting off food and fuel supplies and deliberately bombing schools, mosques and hospitals to crush morale. There have even been reports of air strikes that target rescue workers responding to an earlier attack. When an area becomes totally besieged, even humanitarian aid is not allowed in, and no one can leave. There have been attempts in the past at temporary **ceasefires** to allow deliveries of food and medicine, but saving the people of Syria has become increasingly difficult.

As the war has dragged on, rebel groups, aid workers and civilians have all issued desperate pleas via social media to foreign governments, the UN, and the public, asking for humanitarian aid and safe passage. In the United States and Europe, people have also asked their governments to be accountable to the people of Syria. Ordinary people have collaborated to raise funds or to gather donations of food, clothing and medical supplies. Organizations such as the UN and International Red Cross, as well as many charities, have been delivering humanitarian aid through the most direct routes from across borders in northern Syria. They bring basic provisions, and they work to improve shelters and access to safe water supplies. In 2016, for example, the UN gave food to 5.7 million Syrians every month. With no peace settlement in sight, humanitarian organizations are struggling to keep up with the growing demand.

Aid-delivery operations are also carried out from Damascus with the consent of the Syrian government. However, in recent months, the regime has banned aid operations in rebel-held areas. Getting aid to people inside the country is becoming increasingly difficult and dangerous. Roads are blocked, and regular routes are becoming untenable. In September 2016,

A shipment of humanitarian aid is loaded onto a military airbus. Will it reach its destination and those who are desperate for its supplies?

The UN coordinates humanitarian relief for those in need, but it has faced many obstacles in its efforts to help the people of Syria.

Russia and the United States brokered a seven-day ceasefire to allow aid into some of the most desperate parts of Syria, but this truce broke down when a convoy of aid trucks and a warehouse for humanitarian aid was hit by an air strike. No one claimed responsibility for the air strike, and the UN was forced to stop all aid operations in Syria.

The intervention of international powers has also thwarted the humanitarian effort. In December 2016, for example, Russia and China vetoed an attempt by the UN to call a seven-day ceasefire in Aleppo, intended to allow humanitarian aid into the city. These were the sixth and fifth times respectively that Russia and China had blocked a UN resolution on Syria. They argued that ceasefires allow fighters to regroup and reinforce their ammunition, which will only worsen the suffering of civilians. For the desperate Syrians in need, there is no time to wait for the resolution of these political differences.

31

Although the catalyst for civil war began in Deraa, in the south of the country, by July 2012, the fighting had reached Aleppo in the north. This city became one of the main battlegrounds of the conflict. Four years of fighting – one of the longest sieges of modern times – left more than 30,000 people dead.

Before the civil war, Aleppo was Syria's biggest city, with a population of about 2.3 million people. Inhabited since the sixth century BCE, Aleppo lies just 50 kilometres from the Turkish border. The city became a prime location for industry and finance, and it was considered an important source of supply lines for food, fuel and weapons of war. As the fighting spread, the city became roughly divided in half. The rebels mainly had control of the east, while government forces had control of the west. Hundreds of thousands of people fled their homes to escape the fighting. Then, in July 2016, government troops, with the support of Russian air strikes, cut off all supply routes into eastern Aleppo. Roughly 250,000 people (one-third of which were children) became trapped in the city. These were mainly the poorest families – the ones who could not afford to get out in the early stages of the war.

In the months that followed, the rebel forces fought back, but failed to break the siege. The fighting was unrelenting. Over 23–25 September 2016, for example, 200 air strikes reportedly hit Aleppo in one weekend. By December, the Syrian Army, backed by Iranian fighters and Russian air power, had captured 90 per cent of eastern Aleppo. On 22 December 2016, the government announced it had taken back control of the city, ending more than four years of rebel rule there. This was a significant moment in the civil war because it gave the government control over Syria's four largest cities. However, the war is far from over. Rebels still control many parts of the country, as do other groups involved in the conflict.

Some residents of Aleppo have now returned and are trying to rebuild their lives among the rubble and devastation.

EYEWITNESS

In December 2016, about 8,000 Syrian families were evacuated from eastern Aleppo on government buses, when Russia and Turkey brokered a temporary ceasefire to aid their escape. Some children had to leave without their parents. Here, a boy, whose name has been changed to Shihab to protect his identity, talks about his experience of fleeing war-torn Aleppo:

These children are now living in a warehouse in the industrial district of Aleppo.

"We feel humiliated for being forced to leave our homes. But we had no other choice... There are no words to describe what it was like and how we felt... People came with their luggage, whatever they could bring with them. But there was no space. People had to leave their belongings lying on the road just to get on the bus. Later that night, it became cold, and to keep warm, people started fires with their luggage. I was one of those who burned their belongings just to feel warmer. I kept only two sets of clothing... Every single person from Aleppo is in shock. The bombings have affected everyone. Evacuating has only made it worse."

What would it feel like to leave your home, not knowing when (or if) you will return?

If you were forced to burn your belongings to keep warm, is there anything you would try to keep?

Why does Shihab think that evacuating has made things worse?

33

CHAPTER 6

THE WAR CONTINUES

With the fall of Aleppo, the war in Syria has entered a new phase. The rebel forces, at least in the form in which they came to prominence in 2011, have not succeeded in overthrowing the government. However, the war is far from over. Much remains to be resolved, both in the conflict itself and in what the future holds for the war-torn nation.

Many Syrians fear further acts of retaliation from Assad's forces. There are concerns that government troops will now turn their attentions to Idlib, where thousands of refugees from Aleppo have been evacuated. IS remains a threat, with control of many areas. Human rights issues are also coming to the world's attention. International organizations and governments are beginning to build cases for potential war crimes, and it remains to be seen how both sides of the conflict stand up to these accusations. In February 2017, a report by Amnesty International shocked the world when it revealed that up to 13,000 prisoners had been hanged in a Syrian government prison over the past five years.

As the Syrian war continues, will Idlib suffer the same fate as Aleppo?

The world waits to see how the policies of the US administration will affect the course of the war in Syria.

Many victims were believed to be civilians who opposed government rule. President Assad denied the findings.

With Syria's fate increasingly tied to the actions of other nations, the war is unlikely to see immediate signs of resolution. With each passing year, the situation in the global community has also changed. For example, the new US president, Donald Trump, could dramatically affect the course of the war if he cuts US support for rebel groups. Lessons have also been learned from the past: although there may be a continuation of limited air strikes, there is unlikely to be an Iraq-style invasion or prolonged Western intervention in Syria.

Despite the difficulties in Syria, many parties are continuing to push for some kind of closure. Peace talks in Kazakhstan and Geneva in the early months of 2017 were designed to build on a nationwide ceasefire called at the end of 2016. This ceasefire is partially holding. It may take many months, but there is real hope that with sustained co-operation and dedication by all parties, Syria can begin to find the road to recovery.

There is no accurate estimate for the economic cost of the ongoing war. In March 2016, President Assad said the war had cost his government more than £145 billion. Both Russia and the United States have also spent millions of pounds a day on operations in Syria. According to World Vision International, if the war ends in 2020, it is estimated that the cost of the conflict will grow to £1 trillion. Humanitarian aid has also been hugely expensive. The UN, for example, anticipated that it would take £5.6 billion to meet the urgent needs of the most vulnerable Syrians in 2016. The level of destruction to the country's infrastructure is also unprecedented. A preliminary World Bank-led assessment in six Syrian cities (Aleppo, Daraa, Hama, Homs, Idlib, and Latakia) showed an estimated £2.6 to £3.3 billion in damage at the end of 2014. Although these financial considerations are shocking, the humanitarian impact of the crisis is unimaginable. Nearly half a million people have been killed, and more than 11 million people – half of Syria's pre-war population – have been forced to flee their homes. Almost 5 million of these have fled the country.

With towns and cities destroyed, rebuilding Syria after the war will be a lengthy and difficult process.

These young Syrian refugees are studying in Turkey, but many have missed out on the chance to learn and create a future for themselves.

The long-term social cost of the conflict is also a consideration. The UN estimates that more than two million children in Syria are missing out on an education. Schools have been destroyed, children stay at home for safety and many teachers have left the country. Some refugee camps provide schools, but there are rarely enough places for all the children living there. In Lebanon, for example, 138,000 children out of 338,000 children do not go to school.

The country has also lost much of its history and heritage – ancient architecture and so much of what Syrians regard as their homeland. Neighbouring countries are suffering, too. Turkey, Lebanon, Jordan and Iraq have borne the brunt of the refugee crisis. The World Bank estimates, for example, that the influx of more than 630,000 Syrian refugees has cost Jordan more than £1.8 billion a year. As one of the most water-deprived countries in the world, these numbers have put a severe strain on Jordan's ageing water system. Lebanon, a country whose population is just 4.5 million, currently has the highest proportion of refugees of any country in the world – one in five people in Lebanon is now a Syrian refugee – and the strain on the country has been overwhelming. As a result, tensions have risen between refugees and their host communities.

One thing that has remained constant throughout the Syrian conflict is the solidarity of the Syrian people in the face of adversity. Millions have suffered the trauma of war and been denied a homeland, but they have remained steadfast in their sense of their identity, and their desire to help their fellow citizens both at home and abroad.

One such person is the Toy Smuggler of Aleppo. Rami Adham was born in Syria but immigrated to Finland when he was 17. Now a father of six, he was inspired to help the children of Syria when civil war struck. Rami makes the journey to his homeland every two months, carrying 80 kilograms of donated toys. He has now visited almost 30 times and delivered more than 20,000 toys. Each journey takes about six weeks to prepare, and some trips require him to walk for up to 16 hours. The Syrian borders with Turkey and Jordan are now closed, so Rami has had to find alternative routes into the country as the "Toy Smuggler".

In 2016, the world's attention was turned to the Refugee Olympic Team, which made history at the Rio Games. The youngest member at eighteen was Yusra Mardini, a freestyle swimmer originally from Damascus. A year before, Yusra and her sister had fled Syria, enduring a 25-day journey to Germany.

Syrian children miss the toys they are forced to leave behind. Rami's actions help bring joy back to their lives.

The 2016 Olympic Games featured the first Refugee Olympic Team, shown here in a mural painted on the streets of Rio.

Smugglers took them across the Mediterranean Sea in a dinghy with 18 other passengers, many of whom could not swim. When the engine failed and they were stranded, Yusra, her sister, and two other passengers swam for three hours to drag the boat to shore and safety. Thanks to their bravery, everyone survived. Since competing in Rio, Yusra has used her fame to address world leaders in a bid to keep the plight of refugees high on the political agenda.

Perhaps the youngest of all is Bana al-Abed, a seven-year-old girl from eastern Aleppo who, with the help of her mother, used a Twitter account to give the world a glimpse of her life under siege. The account had more than 350,000 followers. Bana's home was destroyed by an air strike in November 2016, but she was safely evacuated from the city and is now living with her family in Turkey. As well as capturing the world's attention, Bana has also used her fame to tweet world leaders, such as President Putin, President Trump and Bashar al-Assad.

These are just a few of the stories that have made headlines, but for each of these inspiring feats, there are many more untold tales.

By the time the war ends, many Syrians may have settled in a new country and started to secure a future there. This will make returning to peacetime Syria a difficult choice. Some Syrians, however, remain steadfast in their desire to return to their homeland and to help rebuild the nation of which they are so proud. After living most of their young lives on the run from war, Syria's youth must wonder when they will return or what home will be left for them to go back to. The war has put their lives and dreams on hold. They have become a "lost generation". Despite these sacrifices, many young Syrians long to finish their education, so they can realise their dreams and make a lasting contribution to their homeland.

As well as emergency humanitarian aid, the UN and donor governments are funding long-term programmes that address the underlying causes of the Syrian conflict, in the hope of rebuilding and promoting peaceful communities. Helping Syria's youth is a top priority for many aid agencies that recognize the strength and potential of this lost generation. Rebuilding Syria's infrastructure, for example, will take a long time once peace is achieved, but perhaps Syria's youth could be the ones to

Many Syrian families around the world are helping refugees from their homeland settle in a new country.

engineer a new nation and mentor the children who follow in the shadow of the war. By turning their back on war, Syria's youth could help leave a legacy of peace.

Humanitarian agencies are also helping host communities and refugees work together to ease tensions and find solutions to limited resources. Some communities are afraid to accept refugees because they are Muslim, who they associate with terrorism, but education can help address these misunderstandings. Refugees are people who once had fulfilling lives with ambitions and plans. The Syrian people have shown a resolve and strength of character that gives them the hope of one day rebuilding all that they have lost.

EYEWITNESS

The young people of Syria could one day help to rebuild their homeland.

Sixteen-year-old Amina from Damascus had dreams of becoming a doctor and finding a cure for AIDS. When life in Damascus became too dangerous, her family fled to Jordan. Although she was able to finish school there, her family can no longer afford to send her to college. Amina is putting all her energy into teaching herself and helping to teach refugees around her. She says:

"What can I do? Grab a weapon and fight? With whom? It's useless. If I returned to Syria now I would be powerless and worthless. I can't do a thing... My brothers and sisters and I want to learn, so we will be able to help rebuild Syria. I believe that I will return one day. But if I return now, and I haven't finished my studies, I can do nothing."

Why does Amina consider herself to be powerless?

How do you think the effects of war and becoming a refugee have affected Amina's own sense of worth?

What is the power of education that Amina is talking about?

41

With so many groups involved in the fighting, and nations unable to agree who should control the country, it is no wonder that peace talks on Syria have taken so long. During the course of the conflict, there have been numerous attempts at peace talks and agreements, but none have proved fruitful. Countries have suggested talks between the Syrian government and the opposition, but it has been difficult to bring both parties to the negotiating table.

The UN has brokered peace talks and plans, each time offering the hope that both sides will comply, only to be met with new signs of war. Countries have also brokered ceasefires in a bid to save civilians and to bring enough calm to the country to allow political negotiations to begin. Time and time again, these have been broken with signs of aggression and one side claiming that the other was not following by the rules.

At a meeting of the International Syria Support Group (ISSG) Ceasefire Task Force, countries express their support for an end to the violence.

Astana, Kazakhstan, held Syrian peace talks in January 2017, when both sides of the conflict sat at the negotiating table for the first time.

INTERNATIONAL MEETING ON SYRIAN SETTLEMENT
Astana, January 23-24, 2017

#Peace4Syria #AstanaProcess #Peace4S stanaProc eace4Syria #Ast Peac

In September 2016, for example, Russia and the US brokered a ceasefire while jointly agreeing to attack IS. When US-led coalition air strikes hit Syrian government troops by accident, President Assad declared the ceasefire to be broken. Towards the end of 2016, Russia, Turkey and Iran brokered a more widespread ceasefire between government troops, the FSA and many rebel groups, but there was still disagreement about the areas it covered. IS and other extremist groups were notably absent, and sporadic fighting brought accusations of ceasefire violations. There may be a temporary truce, but it is fragile.

In January 2017, peace talks in Astana, Kazakhstan, were a major step forward, when the Syrian government and parts of the opposition met face-to-face at the negotiating table for the first time. IS were not part of the consultation. After the talks, Russia drafted a future constitution for the country, but the plan did not specify President Assad's role. This still remains a contentious issue. The rebels insist he must leave power, while Assad's supporters want him to remain in office. The rebels also refused to participate in direct talks over ceasefire violations.

With neither side able to defeat the other, nor agree on the future, most nations believe the best hope of peace is to work out a political arrangement between the warring parties, accompanied by a ceasefire and a process of reconstruction. Whether different factions can agree on the finer details of a new Syrian state remains to be seen. Without political arrangements in place, it will be difficult to maintain a ceasefire. All these milestones will need to be taken in the context of a collective counterterrorism effort, too.

Even when the guns stop firing and the bombs fall silent, it will take years for Syria to rebuild its future. Any peace deal will not automatically solve the country's problems. The safety and stability of the nation depends on a sustained collaborative effort by all parties involved. With nearly 5 million Syrians having fled the country, there will be fewer people to rebuild the nation. However, many have vowed to return one day to contribute to the country of which they are so proud, and there is the hope of a new generation. For the first time in history, personal stories from the conflict have reached all corners of the globe via the internet and social media. Could this knowledge bring the power of a collective voice that ensures the Syrian situation is resolved and not forgotten?

One of the underlying causes of the conflict was a simple struggle for dignity. When ordinary people took to the streets in 2011, their peaceful

protests were seeking basic human rights. Who could have foreseen that a desire for freedom would lead to six years of devastation and violence? Nearly half a million people have lost their lives, more than 11 million have lost their homes, and a whole generation of young people has lost its dreams and futures. But with a collaborative effort, perhaps Syria will one day rise again, and this dreadful chapter in the nation's deep and valued history will be a lesson to us all.

The people of Aleppo protested for freedom, but now every day is a struggle for survival.

WAR STORY

To find out more about the Syrian civil war and to consider some of the issues raised by the conflict, write your own "eyewitness" account of an event during the crisis.

1. Which event will you write about? Perhaps you could choose the protests in Deraa, the Battle for Aleppo or the journey of a refugee to Europe.

2. Research your chosen event using books in your school and local library. With the help of an adult, you could search the internet. Be aware that many websites about the Syrian civil war contain graphic images and information.

3. From what point of view will you write your account? You could choose a parent, child, soldier, doctor, charity worker or politician, for example.

4. What form will your account take? It could be a piece of journalistic writing (as on page 9), a recollection of events (as on pages 27 and 33), a letter, a report or a diary entry.

GLOSSARY

aides assistants to a political leader

air strikes attacks made by aircraft

asylum protection granted by a state to someone who has left their country as a refugee

authoritarian enforcing strict obedience to a leader at the expense of personal freedom

besiege surround with armed forces in order to capture it or force its surrender

caliphate an Islamic state led by a caliph, a political and religious leader believed to be a successor to the Islamic prophet, Muhammad (pbuh)

civilians people who are not in the armed forces or police force

civil war war between organized groups in the same country

collective punishment form of retaliation where the friends and relatives of a suspect are also targeted

Crusades Medieval military expeditions made by Europeans to reclaim land from Muslims in the 11th, 12th and 13th centuries

displaced when someone is forced to leave their home, because of war, persecution or natural disaster

ethnicities social groups that have a common national or cultural tradition

evacuated moved from a dangerous place to a safe place

extortion obtaining money through force or threats

factions small organized dissenting groups within a large political group

humanitarian concerned with preventing human suffering

infidels people who do not accept the Muslim faith

militias military forces raised from the civil population for the purpose of a particular combat situation

Muslim Brotherhood Islamic religious and political organization, founded in Egypt in 1928, that seeks to establish a nation based on Islamic principles

napalm highly flammable jelly used in bombs and chemical weapons

Nobel Peace Prize prize awarded annually worldwide for excellent achievements in world peace

political autonomy ability to self-govern without the control of another

propaganda information used to promote a particular point of view

refugee person forced to leave his or her country, often due to conflict

retreat withdraw

sarin extremely poisonous gas used in chemical weapons

United Nations (UN) international organization with 193 independent states as members

war crimes severe human rights violations, such as murder, rape and massacres

FIND OUT MORE

BOOKS

Far From Home: Refugees and migrants fleeing war, persecution and poverty, Cath Senker (Franklin Watts, 2017)

Leaving My Homeland: A refugee's journey from Syria, Helen Mason (Crabtree Publishing Company, 2017)

Refugees and Migrants (Children in Our World), Ceri Roberts (Wayland, 2016)

Welcome to Nowhere, Elizabeth Laird (Macmillan Children's Books, 2017)

WEBSITES

BBC News
www.bbc.co.uk/news/world-middle-east-35802955
How do Syrian children explain the war? Listen to some of their stories on the BBC website.

UNICEF UK
www.unicef.org.uk/syria-children/
Find out more about how UNICEF is working to help the children of Syria.

World Vision
www.worldvision.org/refugees-news-stories/syrian-refugee-crisis-facts
Read refugee's stories, listen to podcasts and learn more about how the civil war is affecting people in the region.

INDEX

Acknowledgements:

The publisher would like to thank the following people for allowing us to use their material:

p9 Abdulhamid Qabbani, "What do Syrian refugees think about their country's crisis?" 24 June 2015, the British Council, www.britishcouncil.org, p15 Shafiq Harris, Kurdish Aid Foundation, http://kurdishaid.help, p21 Nadia Murad, www.nadiamurad.org, p27 Walaa, "Syrian refugee mother struggles to reunite her family" 7 July 2016, Mercy Corps, www.mercycorps.org.uk, p33 Shihab, "Fleeing Aleppo: one family's story of leaving the war-torn city" 19 December 2016, World Vision, www.worldvision.org.uk, p41 Amina, "Amina's story: I still have hope" 1 March 2016, Mercy Corps, www.mercycorps.org.uk.